THE FIVE RITES FOR COMPLETE BEGINNERS

The Step by Step Guide on Strong Five Tibetans Exercises to Boost Energy, Power, Increase Health, Anti Aging and Longetivity

Gaston Harry

Copyright@2020

TABLE OF CONTENT

CHAPTER 1 3
   Introduction 3
CHAPTER 2 5
   What are the 5 Tibetan Rites? 5
CHAPTER 3 7
   What are the focal points? 7
CHAPTER 4 19
   Wellbeing tips 19
THE END 31

CHAPTER 1

Introduction

The Five Tibetan Rites are an outdated yoga practice that contains a game plan of five exercises performed multiple times every day.

Experts report that the program has various physical, mental, and significant focal points.

On account of these points of interest, the Five Tibetan Rites are by and large known as the "Wellspring of Youth."

We ought to research what the five Ritess are, the methods by

which to perform them, and
the upsides of this preparation.

CHAPTER 2

What are the 5 Tibetan Rites?

The Five Tibetan Rites are accepted to be more than 2,500 years old. They were evidently made by Tibetan lamas (ministers), or heads of Tibetan Buddhism.

In 1985, the Ritess were first familiar with Western culture in the book "Out of date Secret of the Fountain of Youth" by Peter Kelder. This book, which depicts the program as "youthing," explains the exercises in detail.

The demonstration of these exercises relies upon the body's energy. As shown by experts, the body has seven energy fields, or vortexes.

It's said that these fields control segments of the endocrine structure, an association of organs and organs that direct a critical number of the body's abilities, including the developing cycle.

Experts state youth and power can be refined when these energy fields turn at a comparative rate. People practice the Five Tibetan Rites to achieve this.

CHAPTER 3

What are the focal points?

There's confined investigation on the benefits of this preparation. Overall, they're established on rambling reports by specialists of the Five Tibetan Rites and the appraisals of clinical specialists and yoga instructors.

Reported preferences include:

help from joint desolation and strength

improved strength and coordination

better scattering

reduced pressure

better rest

improved energy

a youthful appearance

Section 4

Guidelines to do the 5 Tibetan Rites

While each custom is expected to be cleaned multiple times every day, you can begin by doing them less regularly.

During the essential week, practice each ritual multiple times every day. Add 2 redundancies for each ritual the following week. Continue adding 2 reps for each ceremony consistently until you're finishing 21 rounds of each ritual reliably.

ceremonies 1

The inspiration driving the primary Rites is to quicken the

chakras. It's customary for juveniles to feel dazed during this movement.

Stand upstanding. Stretch your arms outward until they're comparing with the floor. Face your palms down.

While staying in a comparable spot, continuously turn your body a clockwise way. Without bowing your head forward, keep your eyes open and cast toward the ground.

Do 1 to 21 emphases.

Turn similar number of times as you can, yet stop when you

feel fairly confounded. You'll have the choice to turn more as time goes on. It's ideal to avoid excessive turning, which is said to overstimulate the chakras.

ceremonies 2

During the ensuing ceremonies, it's fundamental to practice significant melodic unwinding. You ought to continue with a comparative breathing model in each emphasis.

To do this Rites, you'll need a covered floor or yoga tangle.

Lie level on your back. Detect your arms at your sides, palms on the floor.

Take in and lift your head, pushing your jaw toward your chest. At the same time raise your legs straight up, keeping your knees straight.

Inhale out and continuously cut down your head and legs to the starting position. Relax up the total of your muscles.

Complete 1 to 21 emphases.

In case you experience issues fixing your knees, turn them differing. Endeavor to fix them each time you play out the Rites.

Customs 3

Like the ensuing Rites, the third rituals requires significant melodic unwinding. You can moreover practice this rituals while closing your eyes, which causes you concentrate interior.

Bow on the floor, knees shoulder-width isolated and hips changed over your knees. Fix your trunk and recognize your palms on the back of your thighs, under your rear.

Take in and drop your head back, bending your spine to open your chest.

Inhale out and drop your head forward, pushing your facial structure toward your chest. Keep your hands on your thighs during the entire Rites.

Do 1 to 21 redundancies.

Ceremonies 4

The fourth Rites, on occasion called Moving Tabletop, is similarly gotten done with cadenced unwinding. Your hands and heels ought to stay set up during the entire exercise.

Sit on the floor and expand your legs straight ahead, feet shoulder-width isolated. Put your palms on the floor at your sides, fingers looking forward. Fix your trunk.

Drop your facial structure toward your chest. Take in and carefully drop your head back. Simultaneously lift your hips and turn your knees until you're in a tabletop position, with your head gently slanted back. Arrangement your muscles and hold your breath.

Inhale out, extricate up your muscles, and re-appearance of starting position.

Complete 1 to 21 emphases.

Rituals 5

The fifth Rites incorporates both the Downward-Facing Dog and Upward-Facing Dog presents. Thus, it's routinely called Two Dogs. This move furthermore requires a steady breathing musicality.

Sit on the floor with your legs crossed. Plant your palms before you.

Widen your feet behind you, toes wound and shoulder-width isolated. Fix your arms and bend your spine while keeping the most noteworthy purposes of your legs on the ground. Drop your head again into Upward-Facing Dog.

By then, take in and lift your hips, moving your body into an upside down "V" shape. Push your jaw toward your chest and fix your back into Downward-Facing Dog.

Inhale out and move indeed into Upward-Facing Dog.

Do 1 to 21 emphases.

To help your lower back, you can contort your knees while moving in positions.

CHAPTER 4

Wellbeing tips

Like all action programs, the Five Tibetan Rites ought to be done with care. Start with sensitive turns of events and a low number of reps.

Heart or breathing issues. Preceding endeavoring these exercises, banter with your essential consideration doctor to find they're okay for you to do.

Neurological issues. Issues like Parkinson's ailment or diverse sclerosis can cause vulnerable balance. If you have one of these conditions, these exercises may not be ok for you to perform.

Conditions that cause dazedness. On the off chance that you're slanted to flimsiness, chat with an expert preceding endeavoring the important Rites. The turning development may trouble various conditions, including vertigo, circulatory issues, or ailment from drug.

Pregnancy. The turning and bowing improvements may not be ensured on the off chance that you're pregnant.

Late operation. The Ritess may cause disarrays in the occasion that you've incorporated an operation inside the latest a half year.

The principle concern

The Five Tibetan Rites, or the "Wellspring of Youth," are a movement of five yoga presents. It's a traditional practice that has been refined for more than 2,500 years. People play out these services with the point of restoring youth and growing essentialness.

For best results, it's recommended to regularly play

out these positions. You can do just them or with another movement program.

If you have a clinical issue or are new to work out, make sure to check with your PCP before endeavoring these moves.

As of now, as a second step of the morning plan (yet before breakfast!), plan and edge the lemon detox drink. There are various minor takeoff from such a lemon detox drink and you can mix it up at any rate you need. I have tons more energy on days that I enjoy this the morning and feel light inside my body.

MY MORNING LEMON DETOX DRINK RECIPE:

Take a glass of warm water, add a portion of squeezed apple vinegar (essentially, it should be unrefined, unfiltered) pulverize one new lemon and add a little honey(raw& neighborhood if available) or apple sirup if you can't stand the kind of the vinegar. Similarly, you can add a hint of Cayenne Pepper and cinnamon. Drink it step by step before breakfast and you will plainly feel the differentiation in your body working. The trimmings all together help stomach burdens, fix hiccups, prevent indigestion, helps with weight decrease, ease a touchy throat and lift energy :)

Part 5

Here's the way to do the 5 Tibetan Rites for better physical and mental prosperity

ceremonies 1: Twirling

Stand tall with your arms released up in game plan with the shoulders, your legs together, and your palms peering down. Try to stand up tall (no drooping!) and release up your shoulders.

Turn your full body a clockwise way on various occasions with the look arranged delicately on the ground. After three complete turns, re-visitation of the center end with your hands on your hips to convey any befuddlement.

Customs 2: Leg raises

From standing, go to the floor and lay on your back.

Detect your arms near to, hands past the hips and palms peering down.

On a take in, raise your head, shoulders, and legs off of the ground with your feet flexed toward your face. Imagine that you're making the letter "J" with your body.

On the inhale out, progressively cut down the head, shoulders, and legs to the ground and extricate up the muscles.

Breathe in and complete two extra adjusts.

Rituals 3: Dynamic camel present

Go to the floor and stoop.

On your knees, spread the thighs hip-distance isolated, keeping the arms and hands close by. Your hands should brush your glutes.

Take a take in. On the inhale out, open chest and drop your head back.

On the accompanying take in, round the spine, imploding the shoulders inward. Present the head, crease the jaw to your chest, and scoop in the waist like you're coming into cat pose.

Re-appearance of objective and repeat twice more.

Customs 4: Moving tabletop

Come to sit in Dandasana, or staff present: Sit with your legs loosened up, arms and hands by the side, palms peering down, and fingertips pointing towards the feet (which ought to be flexed).

On the take in, gently raise the hips upward, allowing the head to fall back. Imagine yourself in a contrary tabletop position.

On the inhale out, carefully bring hips down to the floor, tucking the facial structure going to the chest. Make a point to keep the spine in impartial and unwind. Complete with two extra adjusts of a comparative turn of events.

customs 5: Downward canine to upward canine

Sit in Sukhasana or straightforward speak to: a pleasant arranged reflection position with your legs botched.

From Sukhasana, push ahead, place knees on the ground to be in plan with the hips. Arms are medium length isolated with palms facing the ground. Wind the toes under and slowly grow the legs behind you into dropping facing canine.

Drop pelvis to the floor, opening the chest and head upward into Urdhva Muka Svanasana or upward standing up to canine.

On the inhale out, keep toes wound and bring the pelvis back up into dropping canine. Your look ought to show up on the thighs.

Breathe in and continue streaming improvement for two extra adjusts.

Rest in child's stance and repeat twice more.

THE END

Made in the USA
Columbia, SC
24 November 2024